Selections from the early print-newspapers in colonial Calcutta, India.1780-1820: Print, public and the press.

FACSIMILE: A CENTER FOR EARLY PRINT.

Published by

LIES AND BIG FEET

ISBN: 9384281085
ISBN-13: 978-9384281083

CONTENTS

ACKNOWLEDGMENTS

These primary texts allow us access to certain moments in the history of British colonization in India. These newspapers were printed in India, and subsequently formed a sub-imperial realm of print induced print. A fundamental question that keeps on recurring is this: how did the transfer of culture take place? Even as we acknowledge that these early print newspapers had little commentary on the doings of the natives, for they were meant for a readership that was British, and resided in India, we realize that the desire for print was almost fetishistic.

1 THE PRINT INDUCED SUB-IMPERIAL PUBLIC.

THE

CALCUTTA GAZETTE;

OR,

ORIENTAL ADVERTISER.

PUBLISHED BY AUTHORITY.

Calcutta Gazette; Thursday; Vol: LXIX; March 12th, 1818; # 1776.

CALCUTTA

THURSDAY, MARCH 12, 1818.

Voluminous files of Madras Journal, containing nothing of importance which has not already been laid before the public in the Calcutta Prints, are the only communications we have received from the Coast. For intelligence from the interior, however, we have been much more fortunate. By a series of letters from different Officers, dated from the from the 18th to the 22d ultimo inclusive, it appears that the conquest and pacification of the hostile districts go on with all the rapidity and steadiness that could possibly be expected, or almost even desired.

THE CALCUTTA JOURNAL

Political, Commercial, and Literary Gazette.

Vol. IV.   SATURDAY, JULY 11, 1818.

Published Daily, with the exception of Mondays – and accompanied with occasional Engravings, illustrative of Antiquities, Science, and the Arts, -- at a Subscription price of Eight Rupees per Month, and Half a Rupee for each Plate issues.

A Discourse at the opening of the Literary Society of Bombay, by Sir James Mackintosh, President of the Society, Road at Parell, 26th November, 1804.

GENTLEMEN,

The smallest society brought together by the love of knowledge, is respectable in the eye of reason; and the feeble efforts of infant literature in barren and inhospitable regions are in some respects more interesting than the most elaborate works and the most successful exertions of the human mind. They prove the diffusion at least, if not the advancement of science; and they afford some sanction to the hope that knowledge is destined one day to visit the whole earth, and in her beneficent progress to illuminate and humanize the whole race of man.

It is therefore with singular pleasure that I see a small but respectable body of men assembled here by such a principle. I hope that we agree in considering all Europeans who visit remote countries, whatever their separate pursuits may be, as detachments from the main body of civilized men, sent out to levy contributions of knowledge as well as to gain victories over barbarians.

When a large portion of a country as interesting as India fell into the hands of one of the most intelligent and inquisitive nations of the world, it was natural to expect that its ancient and present state should at least be fully disclosed. These expectations were indeed for a time disappointed: during the tumult of revolution and war it would have been unreasonable to have entertained them; and when tranquillity was established in that country which continues to be the center of the British power in Asia. It ought not to have been forgotten that every Englishman was fully occupied by commerce, by military service, or by administration: that we had among us no idle public of readers, and consequently no separate profession of writers; and that every hour bestowed on study was to be stolen from the leisure of men often harassed by business, enervated by the climate, and more disposed to seek amusement than new occupation in the intervals of their appointed toils.... It is not therefore to be wondered at, if in India our national character, co-operating with local circumstances, should have produced some real knowledge of which we had become masters. Yet some of the earliest exertions of private Englishmen are too important to be passed over in silence. The compilation of laws by Mr. Halhed, and the *Ayeen Akbaree*, translated by Mr. Gladwin, deserve honourable mention. Mr. Wilkins gained the memorable distinction of having opened the treasures of a new learned language to Europe.

But, notwithstanding the merit of these individual exertions it cannot be denied that the area of a general direction of the minds of Englishmen in this country towards learned inquiry, was the foundation of the Asiatic Society by Sir William Jones. To give such an impulse to the public understanding is one of the greatest benefits that a man can confer on his fellow men. In such an occasion as the present, it is impossible to pronounce the name of Sir William Jones without feelings of gratitude and reverence. He was among the distinguished persons who adorned one of the brightest periods of English literature. It was by no mean distinction to be conspicuous in the age of Burke and Johnson, of Hume and Smith, of Gray and Goldsmith, of Gibbon and Robertson, of Reynolds and Garrick. It was the fortune of Sir William Jones to have been the friend of the greater part of these illustrious men. Without him, the age in which he lived would have been inferior to past times in one kind of literary glory. ... His writings everywhere breathe pure taste in morals as well as literature; and it may be said with truth, that not a single sentiment has escaped him which does not indicate the real elegance and dignity which pervaded the most secret recesses of his mind. He had lived perhaps too exclusively in the world of learning for the cultivation of his practical understanding. Other men have meditated more deeply on the constitution of society, and have taken more comprehensive views of its complicated relations and infinitely varied interests. Others have therefore often taught sounder principles of political science; but no man more warmly felt, and no author is better calculated to inspire, those generous sentiments of liberty without which the most just principles are useless and lifeless, and which will, I trust, continue to flow through the channels of eloquence and poetry into the minds of British youth.

... But it would be unpardonable not to speak of the College of Calcutta, of which the original plan was doubtless the most magnificent attempt ever made for the promotion of learning in the East. I am not conscious that I am biased either by personal feelings or literary prejudices, when I say that I consider that original plan as a wise and noble proposition, of which the adoption in its full extent would have had the happiest tendency to secure the good government of India, as well as to promote the interest of science. Even in its present mutilated state we have seen, at the last public exhibition, Sanskrit declamation by English youth; a circumstance so extraordinary, that if it be followed by suitable advances, it will mark an epoch in the history of learning. Among the humblest fruits of this spirit I take the liberty to mention the project of forming this Society, which occurred to me before I left England, but which never could have advanced even to its present state without your hearty concurrence, and which must depend on your active co-operation for all hopes of future success.

... I am ambitious of no higher office than that of faithfully conveying to India the desires and wants of the learned at home; and of stating the subjects on which they wish and expect satisfaction, from inquiries which can be pursued only in India.

THE CALCUTTA JOURNAL

Political, Commercial, and Literary Gazette.

Vol. IV.   SUNDAY, JULY 11, 1819.

Published Daily, with the exception of Mondays – and accompanied with occasional Engravings, illustrative of Antiquities, Science, and the Arts, – at a Subscription price of Eight Rupees per Month, and Half a Rupee for each Plate issues.

Literary Society.

In continuation of our endeavours to excite in the public mind, some interest in pursuits that have of late fallen into neglect; to rouse some of the latent sparks of genius, talent, and the power of investigation, which must exist tho' they lie dormant and inactive; and to diffuse throughout the community of India generally some portion of that love of Information, respect of Science, and due estimation of Philosophical Research, which characterises the land of our birth, and gives to Britain the proud pre-eminence that she enjoys over all the nations of the earth; we present to them in our columns of to-day a document which deserves their deepest attention.

We have before given the outline history of the Foundation of the Literary Society, and a list of the Papers composing the first Volume of their Transactions, which has but just reached India. We may add some facts with which we are personally acquainted, as they will tend to show the eminent utility of such an Institution, and the new sources of pleasure that are opened by it to society at large.

...

One portion of the apartments [of the library] are laid out in a splendid Library, comprising at this time probably more than 10,000 volumes. Into this, Subscribers are admitted, with the privilege of introducing strangers without charge for a month. It is furnished with all the popular Journals and periodical works of the day, and the most approved Atlases of maps and charts, with globes, and every other necessary for the gratification of enquiry. Books are taken out by the Subscribers on the usual terms of Circulating Libraries.

...

To this department is attached a Museum of Nature and Art, in which are preserved specimens of the animal and mineral kingdoms in great variety, models of machinery and other curiosities, with philosophical instruments for the investigation of subjects connected with science.

During our stay at Bombay, at different periods in the years 1815, 1817 and 1818, the meetings of this Society were held weekly, for the purpose of reading such original Papers as might have been presented to the Secretary in the interim; and for Literary conversation. These meetings usually assembled at four o'clock, and continued until sunset, ...

As far as our own experience went, these meetings were not fully attended, seldom exceeding twenty, and oftener twelve or fifteen persons; but as these comprised the best informed members of the Society; they were the more agreeable, and the more effectual too, perhaps, from their being thus select.

A meeting never took place, without an original Paper being read, on some branch of Literature: for it is one of the prominent features of the Bombay Literary Society, and that which gives it a decided superiority over the Asiatic Society of Bengal, that any subject within the extensive range of Literature generally, is admitted for discussion, instead of confining it purely to Oriental matter, in which so few are willing to devote the application necessary to excel.

...

After the reading of such Papers, the members present at the meeting are permitted to make their observations on any portion of their contents, and the originals are then handed over to the Committee of Papers, for their determination as to their being printed with the Transactions of the Society.

It is impossible to describe the advantages arising to the Community at large from all this, and more particularly to the younger branches of it; new topics of conversation are suggested, emulation is excited, a habit of reasoning and enquiry is formed, and a taste is established for that which is permanently beautiful and excellent, in opposition to those frivolities which live but their little hour upon the stage, and leave disgust behind them when the charm of their novelty is gone.

...

We should have been happy to have closed this sketch with a notice of some similar Institution among us here in Calcutta. The reputation of the Asiatic Society, the transcendent abilities and refined taste of its Founder, the talents of its succeeding Presidents, and the mass of erudition and accurate research displayed in their valuable labours which are already before the world; render any eulogium on the excellence of this Establishment quite unnecessary. But their investigations are confined to Oriental Literature, and are carried on slowly, with all the patient examination that such abstruse subjects requires, and always in the tranquillity of retirement from the noise and bustle of active or of fashionable life.

THE

CALCUTTA GAZETTE;

OR,

ORIENTAL ADVERTISER.

PUBLISHED BY AUTHORITY.

VOL. VIII.   THURSDAY, NOVEMBER 29, 1787. [No. 196]

To the EDITOR of the CALCUTTA GAZETTE,

SIR,

A MAN who has the least portion of leisure to bestow on the various publications of the day, will not hesitate to pronounce this to the *Poetical Age* – No *Lady* or *Gentleman*, (we have no *men* and *women*) can now experience any of the common accidents which attend our moral Pilgrimage, such as being married, ruined, cuckolded, imprisoned, or hanged; nor enjoy the rational pleasures of dancing, drinking, coquetting, gambling, dressing, etc. but the muses begin their song, and Apollo tunes his fiddle. – The immortal strains are suffered to reach us through the medium of the *fiery energy* of HAYLEY's majestic numbers, the soft *simplicity* and *unadorned* style of the genius SEWARD, and the pretty warblings of the new-fledged WILLIAMS –Bristol sends forth her pipe makers and milk maids, and London trains her pigs to letters, that they also may become the vehicles of song. We are, in short, a nation of Poets – A compensation sufficient to console us for the loss of Empire; and of character, both public and private – At so favourable a juncture, when criticism is exploded as cruel, wit as rudeness, and learning as pedantry, when our taste is purified that a CHARLOTTE SMITH dies unlamented, and her sonnets (worthless because they speak the mere language of nature) lie unread, permit me, Mr. Editor, to contribute my mite to the general stock of rhime, scrawled over a dish of tea in a happy moment of vacuity – Should it meet with a favourable reception, I shall from time to time indulge the pleasing propensity, in hopes that although I may not obtain a seat at their tea-table, yet that I may arrive at the honour of holding up the tails, or carrying the pattens of the muses of my Lords CARLISLE, PALMERTON, or MULGRAVE.

A MADRIGAL.

FOR me my fair a Pudding made,

Where choicest tastes in union meet,

When smoking on the dresser laid,

Its steam gave sweetness to the sweet.

A whelp that to the kitchen stole,

To steal a bone or get a sop,

Beheld it from his lurking hole,

And out the ugly cur did pop.

No more he thought of skin or scrag,

Disdaining all his former prey;

Th' ungrateful spoiler left the bag,

But with the Pudding ran away.

I am, SIR,

Your Humble Servant,

P.P.

FOR THE CALCUTTA GAZETTE

MR. EDITOR,

If you think the following lines, in reply to the Gentleman who appeared in the POET's Corner *of your left, under the signature of* ADMIRATOR, *have any merit, pray insert them.* M.

O THOU whose lofty thoughts disclaim,

The beaten, vulgar track to fame,

Whose bold ambition can dispense

With wit, and laugh at common sense,

Whose fiery Peg – disdaining check,

Regardless of his rider's neck,

Thro' thick and thin explores his way

And kicks at all the critics say;

Thy bold Pindarics clearly prove,

Nonsense, is eloquence ...

A SPECIMEN OF PROFESSIONAL ELEGANCE, in a LOVE LETTER from a LAWYER, to his MISTRESS.

Dear Madam,

The circuit is nearly over, and the Judges and Lawyers on their return home; but no felon sentenced at the Affixes to transportation, could have been in a more wretched state than your humble servant; for I can safely make affidavit, that each day that I do not behold your lovely face, appears a dies mon. Cupid, the tipstaff, has served me with an attachment from your bright eyes, more dreadful than a green wax process. He has taken my heart into custody and will not accept of bail; unless you allow of my plea, I must be non-suited in a cause I have set my heart on. - -Why will you, whilst I pine in hopes of a rejoinder, hang me up term after term by frivolous delays, which tend only to gain time.

CALCUTTA GAZETTE

THURSDAY,   JUNE 18, 1818.   [No. 1790.

'Dr. Brody attempted in verse a translation of the AEnid, which, when dragged into the world, did not live long enough to cry.'

JOHNSON'S LIVES OF THE POETS.

LA HENRIADE,

TRANSLATED INTO ENGLISH VERSE

Apollo and the Muses have long been supposed to exercise an extraordinary

Influence in the Eastern world; poetry and fiction have laid claim to some of its fairest regions; they have been universally acknowledged as the legitimate children of the sun, and no love sick damsel or romantic youth has dared a flight into the higher regions of poesy and sentiment, without drawing a hero or a heroine from the court of Delhi or the valley of Cashmere.

...

We shall trouble our readers with few truisms on the general advantages of translations; every one agrees to rank them, at least, in the second class of literary merit – and we think ourselves, that he who discloses the moral and intellectual treasures of one nation to the knowledge of another , has little less merit than the original author.

16

Our own countrymen have been peculiarly eminent in this respect; our greatest poets have thus employed their talents, they have given us the splendid relics of former times in all the charms of our native language, and Dryden, Pope and Cowper, have added graces and beauties of their own without injury to their great originals. It was long a matter of dispute whether verbal translations were to be preferred to such as transferred merely the ideas and images of an author into a different language. The first translators employed themselves in close and crampt attempts at verbal imitation. .. The other extreme, however is equally faulty, and following up the simile, we might compare the translator of this class to the traveller who describes the habits and manners of Italy and France, without a day's absence from the parish of St. Pauls. Dr. Johnson, with his usual elegance and acumen, thus settles the point, "There is," says he, "undoubtedly mean to be observed – Dryden saw very early, that clearness best preserved an author's sense, and that freedom best exhibited his spirit; *he* therefore, will deserve the highest praise, who can give a representation at once faithful and pleasing – who can convey the same thoughts with the same grace - -and who, when he translates, changes nothing but the language." The object of our author, however, is equally novel and ingenious: like a native tailor he is determined to stick close to his pattern, and he sacrifices both rhyme and reason to get into one line what Voltaire has got before him. ...

We shall make only one other remark on the general questions of translations, and that is, that they are obviously useless, unless they supply a vacuum in literature – other translators have urged as a plea for publishing, their desire to supply such deficiency, or the inaccuracy of a similar performance but here we have an author who gives his version to the public, because *he* did not know when to began it, that there was another in existence. He seems to fear that his veracity may be questioned – he need not – for we feel assured, that had he seen any other translation, he would never have had the temerity to publish his own. ...

There are three things which we consider requisite in making a poetical translation, 1 st, a knowledge of the language *from* which the translation is made, 2dly, of that *into* which it is made, and 3dly, a slight acquaintance with rhyme and meter....

THE

CALCUTTA GAZETTE;

OR,

ORIENTAL ADVERTISER.

PUBLISHED BY AUTHORITY.

VOL. X.   THURSDAY, OCTOBER 16, 1788.   [No. 242]

The DEATH *and* CHARACTER *of the Emperor JEHANGIR,*
from the History of Hindostan, lately published by
FRANCIS GLADWIN, Esq.

In the beginning of March Jehangir set out for Cashmeer. He was now unable to support the summer heat in Hindostan, so that his journey was more a matter of necessity than any of his former ones. He celebrated the festival of the new year on the banks of the Chenab, and the next day proceeded on his journey. Upon receiving intelligence of the death of Mokurrem Khan, Soobedar of Bengal, he appointed Fidary Khan to that government, who stipulated to remit annually to court, five lakhs of rupees for the Emperor, and the like sum for Noorjehan Begum.

While the Emperor was at Cashmeer, he had a violent attack of his disorder, which the physicians apprehended would have been fatal. He, however, recovered from immediate danger, but continued for some time to have such a shortness of breathing, that he found it painful to be carried about even in a Palkee; his appetite was entirely gone, and he even refused Opium, to which he had been accustomed above forty years. He had no inclination for anything but grape wine.

…

Jehangir possessed considerable literary abilities. He added some chapters to the Emperor Baber's Commentaries, in the Turkish language. He also wrote his own Memoirs in the Persian language, containing a minute account of the political and private conduct of his own life, from the commencement of his reign to the end of the twelfth year: they are universally admired for the purity, elegance, and simplicity of the style; and he appears, in general, to have exposed his own follies and weaknesses with great candour and fidelity: when he had completed the memoirs of twelve years, he distributed several copies of them amongst his children, and principal officers of his court.

THE

CALCUTTA GAZETTE;

OR,

ORIENTAL ADVERTISER.

PUBLISHED BY AUTHORITY.

THURSDAY, JUNE 18, 1818.   [No. 1790]

ADVERTISEMENTS.

THE former PROPRIETORS of the CALCUTTA
GAZETTE having disposed of their interest in that

Concern, to Mr. HEATLEY; beg leave to solicit in favour of that Gentleman, the continuance of the same Patronage and Support, which the Concern has hitherto derived from their Friends and the Public at large.

The PROPRIETORS further announce, that they have authorised Mr. M. LUMSDEN to receive and grant discharge for the outstanding Debts, due to the Concern up to the present period.

Calcutta 10th June, 1818.

TO THE PUBLIC.

NOTICE is hereby respectfully given, to the Subscribers to the CALCUTTA GAZETTE, and MORNING POST NEWS-PAPERS, to the Patrons of those Presses, and to the Public in General, that both presses have this day been removed to No. 12, Mangoe Lane, and that the Press formed by their junction will in future hear the name of the UNION PRESS, from which the two above mentioned Newspapers will continue to be issued. The DAILY ADVERTISER will continue as usual.

Calcutta, June 10, 1818.

AS numerous suggestions and applications have been made by Subscribers and others, to have the day of publication of the CALCUTTA GAZETTE changed, the present PROPRIETOR has resolved on transferring it to Tuesday, and accordingly the next number will appear on the 23rd Instant, and Tuesday will thenceforward be the stated day of publication. THE PROPREITOR only has to add, that such arrangements are now in progress, as he trusts, will obtain for this long-established Paper an increasing share of public approbation.

June 18, 1818.

CALCUTTA GAZETTE

VOLUME LXIX.]   TUESDAY, SEPTEMBER 29, 1818. [No. 1805.

ADVERTISEMENT.

TO THE SUBSCRIBERS

CALCUTTA GAZETTE

AND

MORNING POST

NEWSPAPERS,

AND

TO THE PUBLIC AT LARGE.

PROSPECTUS OF A NEW PAPER.

TO BE ENTITLED

THE CALCUTTA JOURNAL,

OR,

POLITICAL, COMMERCIAL, AND LITERARY GAZETTE.

"A forward (sic) retention of custom is as turbulent a thing as innovation, and
they that reverence too much old times are but a scorn to the new." – *Bacon.*

THE state of the Press has been a subject of surprise, of
disappointment and of regret, to all strangers on their first
arrival in India; and tho' the impression of its
imperfections gradually loses its force after a long
residence in the country, yet some of its ablest apologies
and most zealous supporters acknowledge its reform to
be a desideratum.

Within the city of Calcutta alone, there are no less than
nine public Gazettes, each of them offering itself as the
organ of public sentiment, each of them professing to
have the earliest intelligence of great events, and each of
them promising their portion of original disquisition.
With the exception of two or three at most, these Journals
are found however to have no sentiment, either of the
public or of their own, on the leading features of the
times, no earlier intelligence of great events than that
which they have copied from their "brother edition" of
the preceding day, and no more of original disquisition
than has been first echoed from the Prints of Europe to
those of India, and then, in sevenfold repetition, from one
to the other, till the weekly round has been completed.

Yet, amid this balance of novelty, Supplement follows after Supplement, in such a multiplied succession as to induce a stranger to suppose that the influx of new information was more rapid than the Press could keep pace with. Custom has established and bad taste retains the practise of filling up a certain number of closely printed columns, the subjects of which, in the dearth of general news, are indiscriminately drawn from old Files of English Papers already more than exhausted and dilated on to an extreme of tedious prolixity. A mass of heterogeneous matter, often illegible from the smallness of the type and wretched extent [sic] of the printing, is thus daily poured forth from Presses, prefacing their labours by lamenting the barrenness of Indian affairs and the want of local incidents to interest their readers and expressing the impatience with which they are looking forward to long-expected arrivals in order to furnish them with something to say on European politics, at the same time that whole pages of stale and uninteresting documents are raked up to complete the number of sheets required. This waste of labour and materials in preparing that for publication which is seldom read, is however far from being esteemed as arising from a desire to promote the public gratification, that it is not unfrequently complained of by those whose hands these sheets may be literally said to fill, but who have seldom sufficient leisure and never the indication to wade through their voluminous contents.

It is proposed therefore to establish a Journal which shall found its claim to public patronage on an exemption from these defects. The proprietors of the Calcutta Gazette and of the Morning Post have determined to sink these Papers, and to substitute in their stead an entirely NEW JOURNAL, to be published on the same days on which these Prints have hitherto appeared, and to issue from the same Press.

To their present Subscribers they pledge themselves to furnish a Paper in every respect more worthy of their patronage than those which it is intended to replace; and to such persons as may honour them with additional support they equally pledge themselves to fulfil the following engagements:

First. That this Journal shall be published on the mornings of Tuesday and Friday, and continue to be issued from the Press on those days weekly.

Secondly. That it shall be printed on a large Quarto size, on good paper, and in a legible type, and that each number shall consist of eight full pages.

Thirdly. That one portion of this Paper shall contain a Summary of the Political and other News of the day, with Extracts of the most interesting articles from the European Prints. That a second shall record the General Orders of Government, Provincial intelligence Law Reports, and Domestic Occurrences, including the Arrivals at and Departure from the Presidency; with the

Marriages, Births, and Deaths of persons in India generally. Then a third shall enter into Nautical and Commercial Details, including the Arrival and Departures of Ships at all the Indian ports, and of such of those as may be connected with India in the harbours of Europe, Hydrographical and other Notices of a Maritime nature, and such Mercantile Information as may be attainable from accurate sources, with Prices Current of Indian Commodities as frequently as advices may be received of fluctuation in the markets of India and of Europe, the course of Exchange, value of Government Securities, and price of Bullion, ...The remaining portion of the Paper will be devoted to Original Communications, Literary and Scientific Notices, the progress of the Lettres and the Arts, Extracts of the most interesting portions of New and Popular Works, Original and Selected Poetry, occasional Reviews of Books, and early Notices of the latest and most approved Publications.

...

Sixthly. ... and it is confidently hoped that this Journal will thus be found to form a cheaper, as well as a more compendious body of political, commercial, and literary information, than any that at present issues from the Indian Press.

It is a duty which the proprietors owe to the public to make known the foundation on which these professions are made, and to exhibit to their view the means by which they are to be fulfilled.

The first of these is their having placed the management of their Journal in the one hands of a gentleman who possesses a general knowledge of the duties of an Editor, and a particular acquaintance with some of the branches of information proposed to be treated of in their columns, besides considerable experience of most of the subjects which compose the essence of our Public Prints.

The second is the arrangement which will be made for securing a supply of the earliest and best ephemeral productions of the British Press in a regular series direct from England, and of the French and Italian Journals, via Constantinople Baghdad and the Persian Gulf, in one season of the year, and by Alexandria and Suez through the Red Sea in the other, with the latest intelligence from three quarters of the world.

A third is the establishment of the correspondents at different sections in the interior of India, as well as the ports of Ceylon and the Malabar and the Coromandal coasts, extending also to the Eastern Islands and to China; by which, as soon as sufficient time shall have elapsed for their communications to become regular, a mass of materials will be collected, which cannot fail to furnish an abundant variety of interesting information.

...

In the rapid extension of British Power over the faierest portion of the Eastern world, in the daily increase of commercial enterprise and wealth, and in the opening of so wide a field in the researches of literature and science, as we have all witnessed under the present vigorous yet benign government of India, these have been ample subjects to excite our interest and to tempt our speculation.

...

Let those who feel the force of such a truth, and who as members of that community are in some degree involved in its application, stretch forth their hands to assist in the accomplishment of this task. With their aid, the zeal of the editor and the warm co-operation of the proprietors of this Paper will be all that is necessary to complete its means of attaining the superiority to which it aspires. If these are conjointly exerted, the CALCUTTA JOURNAL will go forth under auspices the most favourable; and this appeal to Indian talent to aid it by its contributions, and to Indian liberality to support it by its patronage, will not then have been made in vain.

It is intended to prepare a Monthly Compendium, to be called THE SPIRIT OF THE INDIAN JOURNALS, to contain only Indian News, whether of Policies, War,

Commerce, or Literature, emitting altogether the information coming to us from Europe, as well as Advertisements and matters of a merely local interest, and thus adopting it for transmission to any part of the world. It is conceived that this would be an eligible Paper to be forwarded to England, America, and the Mediterranean; and such persons as may be disposed to secure copies of its first Number goes to press.

THE

CALCUTTA GAZETTE;

OR,

ORIENTAL ADVERTISER.

PUBLISHED BY AUTHORITY.

SEPTEMBER 6TH, 1792.

MR. JOSEPH COOPER.

INTENDS TO OPEN.

ON THE FIRST DAY OF OCTOBER NEXT.

A CIRCULATING LIBRARY.

AND HAS FOR THAT PURPOSE, TAKEN THE HOUSE OF MR. ANDREWS, WHICH WAS OCCUPIED BY HIM WHEN HE KEPT THE CIRCULATING LIBRARY.

PROPOSALS.

I. -- EACH SUBSCRIBER to pay Six Sicca Rupees per Mensem, regularly, on the first of every Month.

II. – Subscribers residing in Town, will be entitled to the use of two different Publications at a Time, an those in the Country to Three.

III. – It is hoped, with a view to general Convenience, that the Subscribers will not detain any Books longer than a Fortnight; and that, in general, they will return them as soon as possible.

IV. – If one or more Volumes of a Set be lost, the whole Set to be charged to the Subscriber who has lost them.

V. – A Catalogue will be delivered at the Time of Subscribing; if another is required, Two Rupees will be charged for it.

VI. – Mr. Cooper pledges himself not to sell any Book in his Catalogue, without replacing it immediately.

Mr. Cooper also promised to procure and add to his Collection, duplicate Sets of all Books in most general Demand, as soon as possible.
Man Ladies and Gentlemen having expressed a desire, for the re establishment of a

CIRCULATING LIBRARY, in Calcutta, and having promised Mr. COOPER their Support and Assistance, he has been encouraged to make a Collection of Books for the purpose; and although they may not, in the infant state of so extensive an Undertaking, meet the ideas of all Ranks of Readers, yet he hopes that they will, for a few Months, make indulgent Allowance for the Difficulty and Expense attendant on the forming a collection; assuring them, on his part, that every Month shall increase it, more or less; and which Mr. COOPER's knowledge in his Professional Line, will make more easy to him than any other Person not conversant in the same Branch of Business.

OLD LIBRARY,
September 6th, 1792.

THE

CALCUTTA GAZETTE;

PUBLISHED BY AUTHORITY.

VOL. IX.   THURSDAY, MAY 1, 1788.   [No. 218]

Madras Courier

THE EDITORS, with best respects to the Public, in proportion to the demand for THEIR PAPER, are sorry to receive from so many respectable authorities, complaints of its unpunctual circulation. They now beg to assure the Public, that they may in future depend on the most exact punctuality for the delivery of the COURIER, and the insertion of ESSAYS and ADVERTISMENTS in that Paper, by application to their present Agents Messrs. HAMILTON and ABERDEIN, Calcutta; or to Mr. JONES, at Messrs. CORBETT and BOYD'S Fort St. George.

Fort St. George, April 5, 1788

N.B.   Such Gentlemen as wish to be supplied with
The Madras Almanac and Civil List, - S.Rs. 6
Or List of the Army,   -   - 10
Or Military Regulations,   -   16

SUPPLEMENT
TO
THE
CALCUTTA CHORNICLE.

SATURDAY EVENING.
MAY 8, 1832.

Bombay

We have to announce to our readers the establishment of a new Gujrathee News Paper called "Jami Jamsheed," which has been set on foot by a Parsee Gentleman, within the last few weeks. It is published weekly, on Mondays, and contains, for the most part, translations of Papers of this Presidency, and commercial intelligence, which cannot fair to make the paper acceptable to a mercantile community like that of Bombay. The extremely neat, and decidedly superior, of that of any the Goojrathee Papers hitherto published at this place – and advantage for which it is indebted to lithography, in which it is executed, and which is much better suited to the oriental character than typography.

In another part of this Paper, will be found an Advertisement acquainting the public that there is for sale a work both in English and Marathee, entitled "an Exposure of the Hindu Religion," by the Revd. Mr. Wilson, being a reply to Morephutt [sic] Dandekar's

Hindu Dharma Sthabana. In the preface to Mr. Wilson's English book, a short account is given of the public discussion which took place last year between him and Morephutt, [sic]... We believe Morebhutt is the first instance of a Brahman coming forwards publicly to vindicate the Hindu Religion and entering the field of public discussion publishing a work in defence. – Bom. Dur.

THE

CALCUTTA GAZETTE;

PUBLISHED BY AUTHORITY.

MAY 21, 1788.

CALCUTTA

CIRCULATING LIBRARY

MESSRS. COCK, MAXWELL, and Co. conceiving that a CIRCULATING LIBRARY on the same plan with that at the Presidency, would be found a great convenience to gentlemen at a distance, who cannot procure Books otherwise than by purchase, and they having now so large a collection on hand as to enable them to divide the same, and yet retain a sufficient number for the use of Calcutta, they propose establishing a LIBRARY at BEHRAMPORE, and also to furnish a Correspondent at DINAPORE and CAWNPORE with Books for circulation at those Stations and in their vicinity provided a sufficient number of Subscribers shall be found to defray the expenses. – And for the accommodation of the gentlemen in the medical line at the different Stations above mentioned, they will furnish a collection of the most approved ancient and modern authors on Medicine, Surgery, Anatomy, and Chymistry.

Should their plan meet with approbation, the Subscribers may be assured that no pains or expense will be spared to render it useful. – The Subscription to be the same as in Calcutta, viz. 8 Sicca Rupees per month.

Public notice will soon be given of the persons who will receive Subscription at the different Stations: in the mean time such gentlemen as may approve the plan, will be pleased to signify the same to Messrs. COCK, MAXWELL, and Co. in Calcutta.

5 ADVERTISEMENTS FOR BOOKS.

THE

CALCUTTA GAZETTE;

OR,

ORIENTAL ADVERTISER.

PUBLISHED BY AUTHORITY.

THURSDAY, JUNE 18, 1818.   [No. 1790]

TO BE HAD AT THE

UNION PRESS,

The New Collection of POEMS,

ENTITLED

BARRACK MUSINGS

IN 1 VOL.OCTAVO.

DEDICATED

BY PERMISSION

TO

Major Thomas Duer Broughton,

Commanding H.C. Eur. Regt.

BY

EDWARD JONES

Private. H.C. European Regiment.

THE POEMS are the efforts of a Bengal MUSE, and embrace a variety of subjects, comprising *Parodies: Sentimental and Descriptive Pieces, Tales, Songs, &c. many of which have elicited applause from distinguished literary characters.*

THE

CALCUTTA GAZETTE;

OR,

ORIENTAL ADVERTISER.

PUBLISHED BY AUTHORITY.

Vol. XIV.   THURSDAY, February 17. 1791.   [No. 364

Asiatick Researches, @c.

WITH ENGRAVINGS.

Just Published,

PRICE FIFTY SICCA RUPEES,

READY MONEY.

TO BE HAD OF

THOMAS WATLEY,

PRINTER OF THIS GAZETTE;

THE SECOND VOLUME

OF THE

Asiatick Researches:

OR

TRANSACTIONS

OF THE

S O C I E T Y,

INSTITUTED IN BENGAL,

FOR INQUIRY INTO THE

History and Antiquities, the Arts,

Sciences & Literature

OF

A S I A.

THE

CALCUTTA GAZETTE;

OR,

ORIENTAL ADVERTISER.

PUBLISHED BY AUTHORITY.

March 28, 1792.

JUST PUBLISHED

At The Calcutta Gazette Office,

(PRICE TEN RUPEES.)

THE SEASONS

A

DESCRIPTIVE POEM

BY

CALIDAS,

IN THE

ORIGINAL SANSCRIT.

THIS BOOK is the first ever printed in *Sanskrit*, and it is by the Press alone, that the ancient literature of India can long be preserved: a learner of the most interesting Language, who had carefully perused on of the popular Grammars, could hardly begin his course of study with an easier or more elegant Work than the *Ritusambara*, or *Assemblage of Seasons*. Every line composed by *Calidas* is exquisitely polished and every couplet in the Poem, exhibits an Indian Landscape, always beautiful, sometimes highly coloured, but never beyond nature: four Copies of it have been diligently collated; and where they differed, the clearest and most natural reading has constantly had the preference.

TO BE PUBLISHED BY SUBSCRIPTION,

A NARRATIVE

OF

THE SUFFERINGS OF

JAMES BRISTOW.

BELONGING TO THE

BENGAL ARTILLERY.

During Ten Years Captivity with

HYDER ALLY and TIPPOO SAHEB.

SUBSCRIPTIONS received at the GAZETTE OFFICE, and the principal Shops in Town.

N.B. WHATEVER profit may arise from this Publication, is intended to be appropriated to the sole benefit of JAMES BRISTOW and his Family, and in order to make the Subscription as general as possible, the price has been fixed at Six Sicca Rupees for Copies Printed on the best Paper, and at three Sicca Rupees, for Copies Printed on inferior Paper.

The Names of the SUBSCRIBERS will be Printed at the end of the Work.

THE

CALCUTTA GAZETTE;

OR,

ORIENTAL ADVERTISER.

PUBLISHED BY AUTHORITY.

SEPTEMBER 6TH, 1792.

IN THE PRESS,

AND SPEEDILY WILL BE PUBLISHED,

Price Eight Sicca Rupees,

THE

T R I A L

OF

Avaudanum Paupiah, Brahmin,

(DUBASH TO

JOHN HOLLAND, Esq.

Late Governor of Fort. St. George,

AND TO HIS BROTHER,

E. *JOHN HOLLAND, Esq.*

Late Member of the Council thereof.)

Of Avadanum Ramh Sawmy Bramin, brother to Paupiah Sunkaraporam Vencatachella Chitty, and Oppeyengar Bramin, for a Conspiracy against David Haliburton, Esquire, a Senior Merchant in the service of the East India Company, under their Presidency of Fort St. George, by force of which Conspiracy he was removed in September, 1789, during the administration of Messrs. Hollands from his stations of Member of the Board of Revenue, and Persian Translator.—of which Conspiracy, they were all convicted at the Quarter Sessions, held at Fort St. George, the 11th, 12th, and 13th days of July, 1792, after a Trial which lasted over 27 hours.

To the Trial is prefixed an address to the Public by Mr. Haliburton, detailing all the particulars which led to the Conspiracy, as also the subsequent Proceedings, and correspondence with the Government, to the time an enquiry was set on foot, which traced this Conspiracy to its source, and enabled Mr. Haliburton to prosecute the Conspirators to Conviction.

N.B. It being the intention of the Editor only to print as many are bespoke, it is requested that those Gentlemen, who wish to be purchasers may send their Names and Address to the Printer. Mr. J. COOPER.

THE

CALCUTTA GAZETTE;

OR,

ORIENTAL ADVERTISER.

PUBLISHED BY AUTHORITY.

| Vol. XIX. | THURSDAY, July 4th. 1793. | [No. 488 |

PROPOSALS

FOR PRINTING BY SUBSCRIPTION.

THE

PERSIAN POETS;

OR, THE

PRINCIPAL WORKS

OF

FERDUSI, SADI, ANVARI, GELALED-

DIN, KHAKANI, NEZAMI,

JAMI, HAFEZ, AHLI,

AND KHOSROU.

WITH

An Account of the Life and Writings of each

Poet prefixed to his Works, from

DEVLET–SHAH.

TO WHICH ARE ADDED,

The following miscellaneous Works, in prose and verses

VIZ. – THE

AYAR DANISH (OF) ABU'L FAZEL,

GULISTAN   (OF) SADI

NEGARISTAN (OF) JOUINI.

THE WHOLE IN THE

ORIGINAL PERSIAN.

From a Collation of the most accurate MSS.

*In the Royal Library in Paris, the Public
Libraries In Oxford and Cambridge, and of
several valuable private Collections.*

WITH

A   G R A M M A R

AND

A   D I C T I O N A R Y.

By the Reverend EDW,
MOISES, M.A.

Trin. Coll. Cambridge;

Master of the Royal Grammar
School, Newcastle Upon Tyne;
and Author of the *Persian
Interpreter.*

CONDITIONS OF THE WORK.

I. The Whole will be completed in FOURTEEN VOLUMES, Double-Royal Quarto. – Price (to Subscribers) TWELVE GUINEAS, if delivered in England; or SICCA RUPEES, 130, if delivered in Bengal.

II. To be printed in the most elegant Manner, on a Talik Type, and a super fine wove Paper. – Each Page to be beautifully decorated with various Ornaments of Figures, Flowers, Festoons, &c.

III. To be put to the Press as soon as five hundred Names are subscribed.

IV. The whole Work to be delivered at Three several Times; Four Volumes within the first Year after the Subscription is filled; Five more the second; and the remaining five Volumes the third Year, or as soon after as possible.

V. Of the very heavy Expense, THREE GUINEAS, or one fourth, to be paid in Advance, (on Subscribing) and THREE GUINEAS, or one fourth more, on each Delivery.

VII. The Names of the Subscribers will be printed in the first Volume.

* * The Price, to Non-subscribers, will be advanced to

EIGHTEEN GUINEAS, in England, or 190 SICCA RUPEES, in India.

~~~~~~

SUBSCRIPTIONS RECEIVED

BY THE EDITOR;

NEWCASTLE UPON TYNE.

THE PRINCIPAL BOOKSELLERS IN

LONDON, BATH, EDINBURGH, DUBLIN,

PARIS, VIENNA, ROME, FLORENCE.

AND BY

MESSRS. LAMBERT, ROSS, AND CO. AND W. SMOULT, IN CALCUTTA.

Who hold themselves responsible to all Subscribers in India, for the delivery of the Books, or to repay them their Subscriptions, in case the Work should not be published.

THE CALCUTTA JOURNAL

Political, Commercial, and Literary Gazette.

Vol. IV.   SATURDAY, JULY 11, 1818.

Published Daily, with the exception of Mondays – and accompanied with occasional Engravings, illustrative of Antiquities, Science, and the Arts, -- at a Subscription price of Eight Rupees per Month, and Half a Rupee for each Plate issues.

Literature

CLAIMS OF PUBLIC LIBRARIES TO THE GRATUTIOUS DELIVERY OF BOOKS.

The claim of eleven libraries to a copy of every new publication, and of every old work re-printed with additions, has occasioned considerable discussion during the last seven years. It has been agitated in Courts of Law, it has occupied the attention of Committees of the House of Commons, it has mingled itself with the lighter themes of social conversations. The question is undoubtedly of considerable importance to literature and literary men. The interests, which are mutually opposed, are each of the highest order. On the one hand, the seats of learning ought to be supplied by some means or other with every source of useful or elegant knowledge: on the other hand, nothing should be done to impair the scanty emoluments of authors, or to diminish the chance of profit to the purchasers of copyright. But the strength of the adverse parties is very unequal. The proprietors of copyright do not return any Members of Parliament; they have no influence over the leading men of State; their might lies solely in the justice of their cause. The Universities have representatives, men of great authority both from their ranks and talents, who cannot feel a bias in favour of the claim of bodies with which they are closely connected, and who cannot lend a very indulgent ear to facts and opinion which they can scarcely assent to, without incurring the imputation of ingratitude, and exposing themselves to the disapprobation of those whose good-will gives them a place, and whose reputation gives them consequence, in the popular branch of our legislature. This direct political power, formidable in itself, is aided by another species of influence, less apparent, though not less effective. The individuals who take an active part in public affairs have, with few exceptions, been educated at one or other of our seats of learning. They of course entertain a natural and amiable partiality towards the pretensions of places where their habits were formed, and their modes of thinking and feeling were determined.

Yet in spite of these powerful advocates and patrons, the public Libraries have lost ground in the public opinion, in proportion as the question has been discussed. ...

Without following the precise order observed either by Mr. Christian or by his opponents, we shall briefly sketch the history of the privilege which has given rise to the present controversy: we shall next inquire into its justice and policy; and we shall then shortly advert to the different schemes which have been proposed for modifying it.

The professed object of the act is to encourage literature; and the method by which it endeavors to accomplish its purpose is by imposing a tax on the publications of books. That this is the real character of the measure, cannot be denied. Mr. Christian himself compares it to the right of tithes: and indeed, all taxes on the production of any article amount ultimately to nothing more than the appropriation of a certain quantity of the commodity to the state without making payment to the original proprietor. Now, if literature is likely to be promoted by increasing the opportunities of readers, may it not on the other hand be discouraged by obstacles thrown in the way of authors and publishers? ...

Since publishers cannot reimburse themselves for the tax by an additional charge upon purchasers without diminishing the demand for and circulation of the book, the loss must fall upon the author- his recompense must be diminished to keep the profits of the publisher at their due level. Are the scanty gains of the writer a fit subject for taxation? Is it decent that the seats of learning should be the advocates for diminishing these gains?

...

Is it not somewhat preposterous that an act, professing to encourage literature, should exact a contribution from the very men by whom alone learning can flourish? – from readers; if not from readers, from writers: and where, through accident, it misses both readers and writers, from publishers, by whom books are circulated and authors excited to activity?

THE CALCUTTA JOURNAL

Political, Commercial, and Literary Gazette.

AUGUST 17, 1819.

Published Daily, with the exception of Mondays – and accompanied with occasional Engravings, illustrative of Antiquities, Science, and the Arts, – at a Subscription price of Eight Rupees per Month, and Half a Rupee for each Plate issues.

Calcutta.— We find that certain cold and freezing apprehensions, which were published here on the abuse of the Liberty of the Press, have been found as well suited to the meridian of Madras, for those who bask in the sunshine of the Government there, and enjoy the full vigour of power --...

In the 117th Number of our Journal, for the 21st of June last, we introduced to our readers the first notice of the work of a M. Gentz, an aulic councillor who had endeavoured to prove that the evils of a free press were greater than its blessings and who cited the *Letters of*

Junius as a proof of the pernicious tendency of public discussions on the character and the principles of those who are set to rule over us. Our own opinions on the subject of the Liberty of the Press were too well known to need repetition; but we cited others at the moment, to prove what was the opinion entertained in England of this contemptible doctrine, preached to free-born and free-breathing Britons, by an enslaved foreigner.

In the India Gazette of the 5ᵗʰ of July, there were published a few columns of remarks on a late British publication, which the Editor professed to have perused, and which was said to contain, "some reflections occasioned by the late sins of the Public Printed," which were "well worthy" as he thought, "the attentive consideration of those who had lately expressed themselves with so much rapture of the Liberty of the Press." The Editor continues to say – "The liberty is unquestionably excellent and refreshing, when not abused; and we, in common with our brethren in this country, enjoy much 'the pleasure of communicating to others what fills our own breast,' although we often find that the power of conception and 'mind's own delight' may exist without the faculty that can make them available for the general benefit."

We have, however, been taught to believe, on the contrary, that the chief pleasure of knowledge is in the privilege of communicating it to others. If this be true of knowledge, it is still more so of feeling, and we are disposed to believe that "the power of conception and the mind's own delight," though they may exist, are of little or no public utility *without* the faculty that can make them available for the general benefit.

We had hitherto conceived that the law of libel, confused and indistinct as it is, with that memorable absurdity for its leading motto, "that the guilt of a libeller is in proportion to the truth of that which he utters," formed manacles and fetters which were sufficiently restrictive of the British Press. But the Editor of the India Gazette thinks otherwise; and after saying that in this publication which he had read, the sins of the public prints in England had been enumerated and exposed with great ability and severity, he adds "If, however, there be any who *seriously desire* to introduce into this country (India) the same freedom which prevails in our mother land, let them read the following description of "a set of men" who now live and prosper among a nation so renowned for loyalty and virtue as the English.

CALCUTTA GAZETTE

LIBERTY OF THE PRESS.

AND

THE RIGHTS OF JURIES.

The confirmation of those Rights, and of that Liberty, heretofore so often violated, but now confirmed for ever was celebrated on the 15th of June, at the Free Mason's Tavern by a very numerous company: The following Toasts were given:--

The Liberty of the Press.

The Trial by Jury,

Mr. Fox, and may the remembrance of his Libel Bill never be effaced from the hearts of the People!

Mr. ERSKINE, and may the Public never forget its obligations to that Constitutional Advocates.

Mr. ERSKINE then rose to offer his acknowledgement to the Company, and observed that nothing was so easy as to make a proper return to a compliment of this kind, particularly when it was addressed to one who had been in the habit of speaking in public. But on this occasion, he confessed he was at a loss to express his feelings with the energy and effect he could have wished.

" I never was so perfectly convinced, said he, as at this moment, that the greatest honour which can be conferred on any man is to be applauded for having defended the Liberty, and happiness to Mankind: but were I now called on to plead for the Liberty of the Press, I believe that at this moment I should be incapable of offering a single word in favour of that noble cause, so much are my faculties annihilated by the pleasure which I feel. - -
…

… I have but one word to add which is, that as long as God shall grant me understanding and ability I solemnly promise …to employ every faculty of my mind not only in the cause of the Liberty of the Press, but in every cause, in every pursuit which tends to the propriety of my Country: yes! To the last hour of my life, will I support every measure that leads to public good, even though my personal prosperity shall suffer by my conduct.

SUPPLEMENT TO THE CALCUTTA GAZETTE

THURDAY, MAY 14, 1818.

THE TIMES, NOVEMBER 21, 1817.

LIBERTY OF THE PRESS.

Baron Pasquier, Keeper of the Seal, then mounted the Tribune and spoke as follows:

"Gentlemen, the project of the law, which we have the honour of presenting to you, ought to exite your attention in a more special manner, because it aims at accomplishing two objects, both equally important. The first is to preserve and secure the exercise of the liberty of the press, consecrated by the charter, by giving to the public authority, the means of separating its legitimate use from the abuse which may result from it; the second, to retain for the Government a protecting power, which you placed in its hands during the last session, and which the political situation of the country still requires, notwithstanding the amelioration in its circumstances.

"The 8th article of the Constitutional Charter is couched in those words: - 'Frenchmen have a right to publish and to cause to be published, their opinions, in conformity, however, with the laws which must repress the abuse of this liberty.'

"Every reflecting mind has admitted, that the liberty of the press would not be complete, and that it could not be enjoyed with entire security, until a law, doubtless difficult to frame, but most indispensable, should provide for the prevention of all its abuses. …"

"It is not necessary, in this assembly, to develop the advantages of the press; you know them; as citizens, as deputies and friends of science, you consider that they are inherent in our rights, and ought to be regarded as one of the surest guarantees for the constitution of the State. … Uncurbed licentiousness would degenerate into confusion and oppression. Such impunity would leave society and citizens unprotected.

"If the writer, who publishes a dangerous work, and one that is contrary in the laws, were not responsible for what he did, the crimes of the press would be privileged; the legislators must use two weights and two measures. …

…

"The liberty of the press may be abused by publishing dangerous or injurious works. Reason and justice require that he who has done the mischief and committed the abuse, should be responsible for them. Thence arises the principle of the responsibility of the author.

ABOUT

FACSIMILE: A CENTER FOR EARLY PRINT AND SOCIETY

Facsimile is an independent research center that works on early print and society in colonial India. It is relevant to remember that print started in Calcutta, India, with the emergence of the East India company in the last two decades of the 18th century.
For more information, please visit us at:
www.colonialprint.wordpress.com

You can contact to us at: earlycolonialprint@gmail.com.

www.ingramcontent.com/pod-product-compliance
Lightning Source LLC
Chambersburg PA
CBHW070647130626

46555CB00006B/2751